A Message from the Lord Mayor

———— ✦ ————

This book is a tribute to some of the fine gems that the First Capital of Upper Canada has to

offer. A glance will give way to unparalleled historical and architectural beauty and share

the past with the future, demonstrating why Niagara-on-the-Lake is the jewel in the crown of

the Province of Ontario.

Michael M. Dietsch

Michael M. Dietsch,
Lord Mayor,
Town of Niagara-on-the-Lake, Ontario

~ HISTORIC ~
Niagara-on-the-Lake

A Pictorial Discovery

by Margaret Dunn

Photography by Michael D. Romanowich

Acknowledgements

This book is dedicated to the gracious and magnanimous people of Niagara-on-the-Lake who preserve the integrity and charm of this unique area of historical and architectural merit.

Thanks to the following for their kind assistance:

Cathy Macdonald, Heritage Planner,
Town of Niagara-on-the-Lake

Bill Severin, Curator,
Niagara Historical Society Museum

Joy Ormsby, Research Chairman,
Niagara Historical Society

Molly Green, Niagara National Historic Sites,
Parks Canada

Frank Hawley,
Niagara-on-the-Lake Heritage Expert

John Jouppien, Heritage Resource Consultant

Peter Stokes, Restoration Architect

April Petrie, Niagara Parks Commission

Keith Fox, Aerial Photography Pilot

Jean Barnes, Project Consultant

Special thanks to my husband, Bill, for his enthusiastic support; to my parents and friends for their steady encouragement; and to Sarah, Scott, Patricia and Geordie for their patience and understanding.

Copyright 1995 Margaret Dunn, Author and Publisher
All Rights Reserved

All Photography by Michael D. Romanowich with the exception of
Page 8 (upper) and Page 9 (upper), both courtesy of Niagara National Historic Sites – Parks Canada
Design by Rose Ellen Campbell, Campbell Creative Services, St. Catharines, Ontario
Map Illustration by Joel Campbell
Printed in Hong Kong by Book Art Inc., Markham, Ontario

Additional copies of this book may be ordered from
Margaret Dunn
7366 Edenwood Court,
Niagara Falls, Ontario, Canada L2J 4E3

Cover Photographs:
Front Cover (A): Hawley House, 392 Mississauga Street
Front Cover (B): Atop 126 Queen Street, a version of the Royal Arms (see page 95).
Back Cover: Mackenzie House and Brock's Monument, Queenston

Canadian Cataloguing in Publication Data

Dunn, Margaret, 1950-
    Historic Niagara-on-the-Lake

Includes bibliographical references and index.
ISBN 0-9699126-0-9
1. Historic buildings - Ontario - Niagara-on-the-
Lake Region - Pictorial works. 2. Historic sites -
Ontario - Niagara-on-the-Lake Region - Pictorial
works. 3. Niagara-on-the-Lake Region (Ont.) -
Pictorial works. I. Title.

FC3099.N54Z57 1995   971.3'38   C95-930110-0
F1059.5.N5D8 1995

Table of Contents

Historic Niagara-on-the-Lake
- *A Pictorial Discovery* -

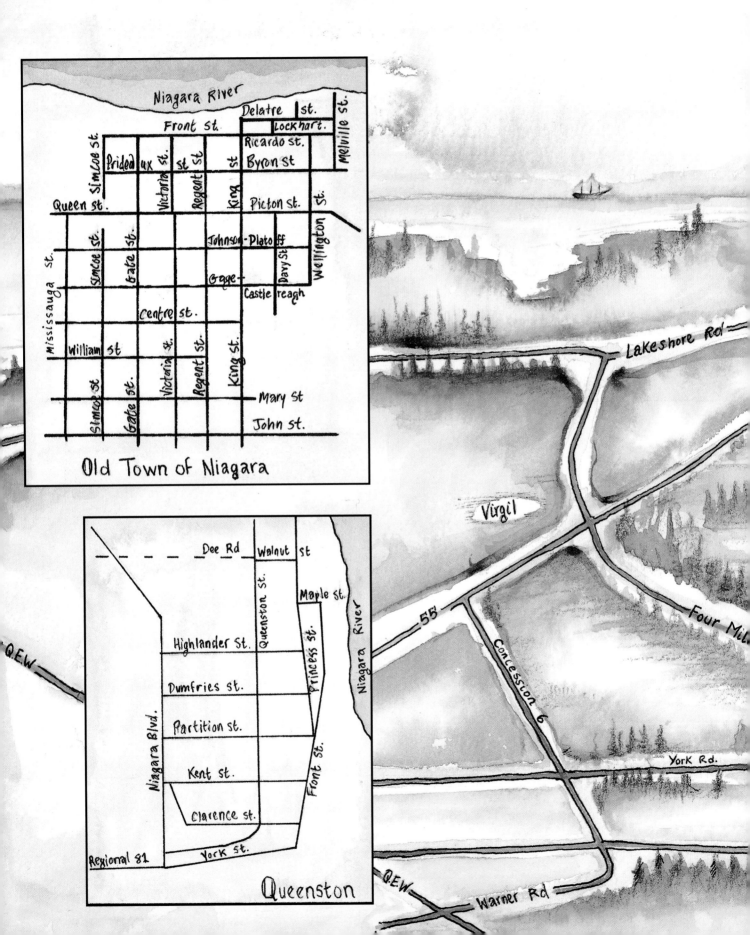

Old Town of Niagara

Queenston

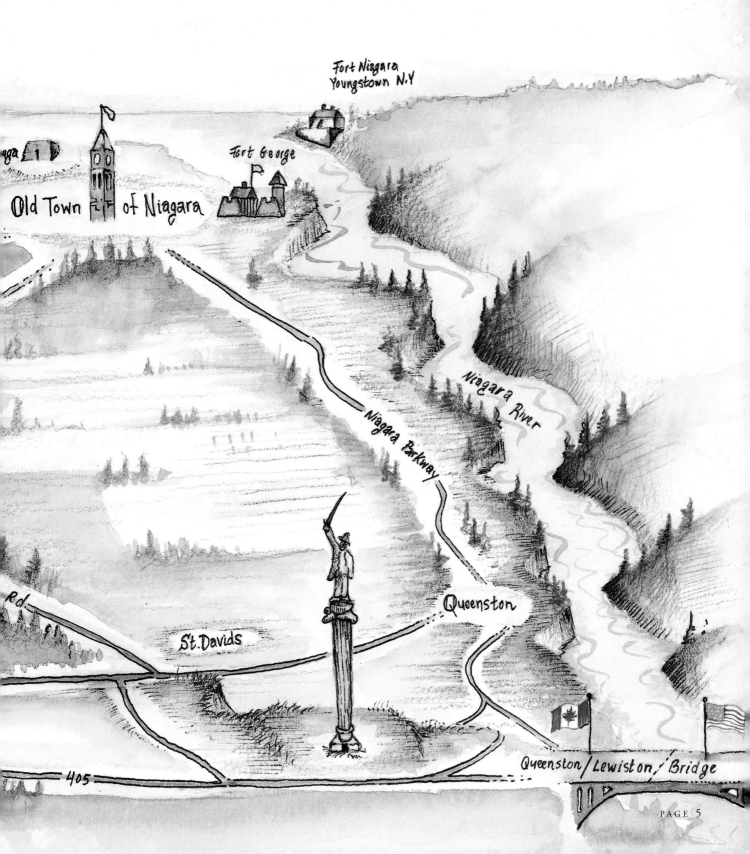

NAVY HALL

When John Graves Simcoe first approached the shores of Niagara by boat in 1792, he expressed disappointment at the sight of the four rundown wooden buildings known collectively as *Navy Hall*. They were constructed in *1765* as barracks, offices and naval equipment storehouses. As the newly appointed first Lieutenant-Governor of Upper Canada, Simcoe and his wife, Elizabeth, left behind a 40-room mansion in England to take up residence here.

Simcoe changed the name of Niagara to Newark and made it the first capital of the new province. Navy Hall may have been the site of the first Parliament of Upper Canada. Although Parliament met only a few weeks each summer, Lieutenant-Governor Simcoe ensured the adoption of British customs and principles of law and government. He was determined that Great Britain would maintain possession of Upper Canada.

The Simcoes rejected the dilapidated Navy Hall building offered to them until it was refurbished two years later. Instead, they pitched tents on the hill above where they enjoyed a beautiful view of the Niagara River and the British garrison at *Fort Niagara* across the river. The tents became widely known as the Simcoe's "canvas house" and served as the birthplace for their daughter Katharine in January 1793. Some years earlier, the tents had been used by Captain Cook on his explorations to the South Seas.

The four wooden buildings at Navy Hall were eventually abandoned. The existing structure was reconstructed and covered with stone.

Above: *Simcoe Monument*

Opposite page:

Upper: *Navy Hall*

Lower: *View of Fort Niagara*

FORT GEORGE

Fort George lies south of the Old Town of Niagara on the high ground above Navy Hall. Built between *1796* and *1799*, it was a replacement for Fort Niagara, which housed the British garrison across the river until 1796. It was also a supply depot and the British headquarters for all of the forts on the upper lakes. The bastions of Fort George afforded a view of the activity at Fort Niagara but proved too distant from the mouth of the Niagara River to provide a strong defense for the town.

Attacks by American artillery during the War of 1812 caused repeated damage to the stronghold. In May 1813 the fort was destroyed by a two-day bombardment from 20 cannons in action at Fort Niagara and another 51 afloat on enemy ships. American troops captured Fort George and partially rebuilt the fortification during their occupation, but the effort was futile. A decade later, Fort George was abandoned and left to fall to ruins.

Only the stone powder magazine survived the War of 1812, but narrowly. It housed 800 barrels of gunpowder when it was hit during the Battle of Queenston Heights. A cannonball passed through the roof and set fire to the wooden supports. While most of the garrison fled the fort in panic, a heroic group of Royal Engineers extinguished the fire and averted destruction.

Built in 1796, the powder magazine is the oldest military building in Ontario. The rest of the fort was reconstructed in the 1930's to appear as it did before 1813.

Both pages: *Fort George*

Below: *Powder Magazine*

FORT MISSISSAUGA

The overwhelming upheaval and destruction suffered by Niagara during the War of 1812 provided the impetus for building a new fort in the immediate post-war years. Enraged by the burning of their houses and businesses, citizens watched as the rubble of their homes and the bricks of an old lighthouse rose in the form of *Fort Mississauga (1814-1816).*

A strategic site was chosen at the mouth of the Niagara River directly opposite Fort Niagara. The central tower, earthworks, and a sally port leading to the water's edge are all that survive of the stronghold. The tower, with walls 8 feet (2.4 metres) thick, was surrounded by outlying log buildings in the shape of a five-pointed star. Fort Mississauga is the only fort of this type in Canada.

Fort Mississauga was to be a permanent replacement for Fort George. Its military purpose gradually diminished, however, following the signing of the peace treaty with the Americans in 1814. British troops were garrisoned at the fort until 1826, then dispersed until the Mackenzie rebellion of 1837 precipitated some repair and rearmament activities. The fort was again manned for action during the tense years of the American Civil War and the Fenian raids in the 1860's.

Fort Mississauga was never attacked.

Both pages: *Fort Mississauga*

BUTLER'S BARRACKS

With the barracks of Fort George in ruins after the War of 1812 and Fort Mississauga under construction, the British chose a site southeast of King Street for their new military headquarters. The cluster of buildings was named *Butler's Barracks*. Butler's Rangers was the regiment of United Empire Loyalists that had assembled at Fort Niagara in 1777, led by Colonel John Butler. Even though the Rangers disbanded in 1784, many of them had settled in Niagara and the name Butler persisted proudly.

The two-storey men's *Barracks (1817)* housed troops that were regularly dispatched to Fort Mississauga. Wives and children shared this accommodation with the soldiers, safely out of range of the American artillery.

A 24-pounder smooth bore muzzle loading gun dating to 1812 sits in front of the *Ordnance Gun Shed (1821)*.

The *Commissariat Officer's Quarters (1817)* is a one-storey structure with a brick kitchen at the rear that was originally a separate building. British officers were expected to live as gentlemen in relative elegance and comfort, even on the frontier.

More than 20 buildings were part of this military headquarters by 1854. The function changed, however, after the Dominion of Canada was formed in 1867. Butler's Barracks was renamed Camp Niagara and became a training centre for Canadians serving in the Boer War, the two World Wars and the Korean War.

This page: *Commissariat Officer's Quarters*

Opposite page:

Upper: *Ordnance Gun Shed*

Lower: *Barracks*

QUEEN STREET

The Old Town of Niagara was a flourishing settlement when the British government created the new province of Upper Canada in 1792. Loyalists from Pennsylvania, New York and Connecticut flocked to the fertile lands at the mouth of the Niagara River, joining settlers from the British Isles, France, Russia and Germany. Niagara's fine harbour became the centre of thriving trade.

Generous one-acre lots in the centre of town were laid out with military precision. Major streets were made 99 feet (30 m) wide, one and a half times the usual surveyor's chain length of 66 feet (20 m).

The Old Town's early prosperity was not to last. Niagara lost its title as the capital of Upper Canada when the capital moved to York in 1797 for reasons of security. The industrial boom based on the town's position at the head of the portage around the falls ended with the opening of the second Welland Canal in the 1840's. Hoping to remain the County Seat, the town went into debt to build the *Court House (1847)*, but the honour went to St. Catharines.

The Court House is a grand building of Queenston limestone. With ornamental windowheads carved in stone, bracketed cornices and a large cupola, it exemplifies Classic Revival architecture. It served as a courthouse until it became the Town Hall in 1862 and later a public meeting place.

The *Clock Tower* at the heart of the Old Town is a striking landmark honouring the fallen soldiers of the two World Wars.

Left: *The Court House*

Below: *Aerial View*

Opposite page: *The Clock Tower*

The Old Town of Niagara

QUEEN STREET

A parade of charming shops flanks the tree lined main street of the Old Town of Niagara. The varied continuous facade of storefronts is a harmonious blend of fine craftsmanship, common scale and richness of detail. While roof forms and upper storey facades vary greatly in style, the prevalence of small vertical upper level windows and mid-19th century details gives them visual rhythm.

Merchants in the early 19th century enjoyed thriving trade that came to the area as the military headquarters and head of the portage route around the falls. Even as early as 1781, the shops offered an astounding variety of goods including Irish linens, fine hats, silver knee buckles, silk mitts, bottles of Madeira, tobacco and books.

A prominently displayed pineapple, the colonial symbol of hospitality, decorates the Gothic Revival storefront of the shop at *16 Queen (circa 1830)*. The upper storey windows have shutters with movable slats to control ventilation and light. The panes reveal an amethyst grey tint which may be attributed to an inferior quality of glass.

The shops at *44* and *46 Queen (circa 1825)* were meticulously reconstructed, retaining the original arcaded brick at 46 Queen.

The Georgian style building at *122 Queen (circa 1840)* complements the Regency style Customs House at *126 Queen (circa 1825)*. A royal coat of arms crowns the structure as it did when William Kirby was the collector of customs for Upper Canada.

Above: *16 Queen*

Opposite page:

Upper: *122-126 Queen*

Lower left: *46 Queen*   Lower right: *44 Queen*

QUEEN STREET

The *Niagara Apothecary* at *5 Queen* is a landmark in the Old Town. Built in the 1820's, it was a barrister's office for many years until it became a pharmacy in 1866. The prominent Sign of the Golden Mortar, a long established symbol of the trade, attests to its operation as a pharmacy for close to a century. The oldest drug store in Ontario is now a museum.

The Apothecary's Victorian storefront with colonettes, cable moulding and Italianate style arcaded windows is an authentic restoration of a Confederation period building.

The former *McClelland's West End Store* at *106 Queen (circa 1835)* earned a venerable reputation selling cheeses, marmalades, teas and goodies for over 150 years. The scrolled "T" above the door is the ancient sign of business signifying tea for sale. The store offered every variety, including "Gunpowder Tea", as listed in the store's account books of the 1830's.

The facade of 106 Queen shows several original details. These include the ornamental fan in the gable, rusticated stone quoins at the corners, and as in the Niagara Apothecary, moulded eaves returns, dubbed "bird houses" by carpenters.

Set amidst a row of bustling shops at *83 Queen* is the *Royal George Theatre (1915)*. First built as a vaudeville theatre to entertain troops during World War I, it became a theatre for Shaw Festival productions. Its pedimented front gable, wide frieze board and Ionic pilasters are classic Greek style.

Above: *83 Queen – Royal George Theatre*

Below: *106 Queen*

Opposite page: *5 Queen – The Niagara Apothecary*

QUEEN STREET

In the Niagara Gleaner of 1817, James Rogers informed the public that his large and commodious house at *157 Queen* was ready to entertain genteel company in handsome style. He added that his liquors were pure and the table supplied with the best the market afforded.

The *Rogers House (1817)* was built on the foundation of an earlier building dating to 1792. Although the Rogers family had relatives among the American officers, they are said to have allowed their home to burn in 1813 rather than show sympathy with the invading forces.

The fine Baroque-Germanic mantelpiece in the parlour at 157 Queen has its own place in history. It is recorded that this family treasure, brought to Niagara by Conestoga wagon, was hauled into the street by Mrs. Rogers just before her home was reduced to ashes.

The Rogers House has typical Georgian features such as the embroidered fanlight and sidelights around the door, but unlike most homes in the Old Town, the door is placed off-centre. The house was originally clapboard over a wooden frame, but was covered with stucco later in the 19th century.

Nearby, *Roslyn Cottage* at *187 Queen (circa 1822)* sits right on the street line, displaying magnificent wood details including fluted pilasters with carved Ionic capitals and modillion cornices. The main entrance and the verandah face the garden. John Davidson's fine craftsmanship is evident in the Greek Revival details.

Upper: *157 Queen – The Rogers House*

Lower: *187 Queen*

Opposite page: *157 Queen – The Rogers House*

QUEEN STREET

The red brick townhouse at *165 Queen (circa 1820)* is remembered as the home of Colonel Daniel MacDougal. He survived a night of suffering in 1814, lying severely wounded on the battlefield at Lundy's Lane.

Typical of homes built along Queen Street in the 1820's, the end walls have a stepped gable and no windows, to allow other homes to be built adjoining. This was done with the expectation of continuing growth and prosperity in the Old Town.

The handsome facade of 165 Queen displays arcaded brick on two levels and an elaborate doorcase. An elliptical embroidered fanlight and sidelights with metal cames and lead rosettes grace the side hall entry. The twelve-over-twelve windows were a popular size at the time of construction, when glass was made by hand in panes of small sizes.

Nearby at *118 Queen (circa 1820's)* is a typical Georgian style two-storey home of the period with a balanced facade, gable roof and end chimneys. Decorative cornices, moulded pilasters, simple sidelights and a high frieze board distinguish the central entry. A blacksmith once kept his shop in a barn behind.

Above: *165 Queen*

Opposite page:

Upper: *118 Queen*

Both lower: *165 Queen*

QUEEN STREET

A spacious home sits well back from the street on a grand estate lot at *228 Queen (circa 1830)*. The two-storey, three-bay white stucco home is of late Neoclassical design. An elaborate Palladian window crowns a handsome entrance. Fine colonettes, pediments, sidelights, and a semi-elliptical transom light focus attention on the entry. The windows display pedimented trim in a Victorian version of Greek Revival.

Like many of the larger homes in town, additions were made in the late 19th century to accommodate the influx of family and guests who enjoyed Niagara as a holiday and cultural centre. Prominent owners of 228 Queen have included the Ryerson family of Toronto and the E.R. Thomas family of Buffalo, New York. The E. R. Thomas Motor Car Company manufactured some of the best early American cars. The most famous was the Thomas Flyer, which won the 1908 New York to Paris Race.

The late Georgian home at *209 Queen (circa 1832)* underwent similar expansion in the late Victorian period. A two-storey extension with spacious verandahs was added to the home. The original nucleus displays the popular hipped roof and balanced facade. A fanlight, sidelights and a Palladian window grace the centre doorcase.

The site of 209 Queen is carved out of the corner of the Fort Mississauga military reserve. A long cellar vault stretching north from the home gave fuel to the popular notion, never proved, that a tunnel once extended to the fort.

Upper: *209 Queen*

Lower: *228 Queen*

Opposite page: *228 Queen*

QUEEN STREET

A spectacular estate home at *284 Queen (circa 1899)* faces Fort Mississauga and Lake Ontario beyond. It hails from the era from 1880 to 1915 when the Old Town emerged as a popular summer resort. Affluent tourists arrived by rail from Buffalo and by lakeboats from Toronto and Hamilton to enjoy fishing and waterfront picnics, homemade ice cream and delicacies from the local shops and farms.

284 Queen was the summer home of American lumber giant Watt S. Lansing, and later was acquired by the Charles Weston family. Both families came to Niagara first as visitors, then as summer residents, and eventually as permanent residents.

Lansing purchased a four-acre block for his estate that had originally been set aside as a clergy reserve. He laid out elaborate orchards and gardens that now form an historic garden landscape with mature trees of many species. Only a fragment of the original lot, along Mississauga Street, was severed from the estate.

Spacious verandahs typical of the Victorian period surround the two-storey clapboard home. A delicate semielliptical leaded glass fanlight and sidelights decorate the main entry, flanked by four pilasters.

The estate at 284 Queen is a fine legacy of late 19th century American residents of the Old Town.

PICTON STREET

The *Prince of Wales Hotel* proudly faces the main intersection of the Old Town at *6 Picton*. Formerly known as Long's Hotel (1882) on the site of a previous inn dating to 1864, it was a prestigious lodging in the late 1800's that welcomed visitors arriving by steamship, stagecoach and a railway that stretched down King Street to the dock area. A visit by British royalty in 1901 gave the hotel its current name.

The three-storey Victorian style inn is distinctive with its mansard roof and bevelled corner. Yellow brick arches and quoins decorate the red brick facade. Additions to the rear and sides of the main block replicate the original colour, style and fine detail.

The *Moffat Inn* at *60 Picton (circa 1835)* was a popular tavern in the mid-1800's and it has operated as an inn ever since. It is a simple Georgian style two-storey building with a gable roof and balanced facade. It displays many of its original twelve-over-twelve windows.

Across the street at *93 Picton* stands *St. Vincent de Paul Church (circa 1834)*. Niagara area Roman Catholics obtained a resident pastor and founded a parish in 1826.

The oldest section of the church is a marvelous example of Gothic Revival architecture, with tall and narrow pointed windows, a wooden vaulted ceiling, and classical pilasters topped with Ionic capitals. A nine-sided front with Gothic windows was added in 1965.

This page: *St. Vincent de Paul Roman Catholic Church*

Opposite page:

Upper: *The Moffat Inn*

Lower: *The Prince of Wales Hotel*

FRONT STREET

The recreational shore now facing Front Street contrasts sharply to the bustling wharf district of the early 1800's. The Niagara Harbour and Dock Company filled in marshy areas, excavated a slip for large vessels, and built a wharf, foundry, shops and warehouses. By the 1840's, more than 350 men were employed building sailboats, barges and steamers.

At the heart of the wharf district was an inn called the "Yellow House" that burned in 1813. The *Old Bank House* that replaced it at *10 Front (circa 1817)* was once the busy Bank of Upper Canada. The basement shows evidence of a vault. The verandah and the stucco finish are likely Victorian era additions.

Colonel Philip Delatre, a president of the Niagara Harbour and Dock Company, once owned the side hall plan, two-storey home at *120 Front (circa 1845)*.

The home at *80 Front (circa 1820)* is thought to have been built for the captain of the Duke of Richmond, a boat that sailed regularly to and from York. A Victorian verandah encircles the long and narrow building. The central chimney accommodates fireplaces on three levels, including the original basement kitchen and slave quarters.

Sea captain Duncan Milloy, who eventually purchased the Niagara Harbour and Dock Company, built a home at *160 Front* in 1824. It became a hotel in the late 1800's, the *Oban Inn*. Following a tragic fire in 1992, the Niagara landmark was rebuilt, modelled on the original structure.

Opposite page:

Upper: *The Oban Inn*

Middle: *10 Front –*

The Old Bank House

Lower: *120 Front*

This page: *80 Front*

BYRON STREET

Lieutenant-Governor John Graves Simcoe hoped to develop a sober, industrious and conscientious populace by establishing the Church of England in the new province of Upper Canada. Reverend Robert Addison arrived as Missionary to Niagara in 1792 and began the ministry with a congregation that included the Simcoes, Loyalist Colonel John Butler and later, Major-General Sir Isaac Brock.

The original *St. Mark's Church (circa 1805)* served as a hospital and storehouse during the War of 1812. Deep scores are evident in the flat gravestone of Charles Morrison, which American army butchers used as a chopping block. When the occupying American forces left in 1813, St. Mark's burned with the rest of the town, leaving only the stone walls.

St. Mark's was rebuilt in a cruciform shape in the decade following the war and expanded to its present shape in 1843. Its cemetery was the only burial site for Niagara's first settlers and was used by all denominations until 1833. Elaborate cast iron railings enclose some of the burial plots.

The *Rectory (1858)* is the only example in town of a Tuscan villa, a style popular then among the well-to-do. Its square tower, round-headed windows, panelled chimney and wide bracketed eaves are typical of the Italianate style.

Above: *The Rectory*

Opposite page: *St. Mark's Anglican Church*

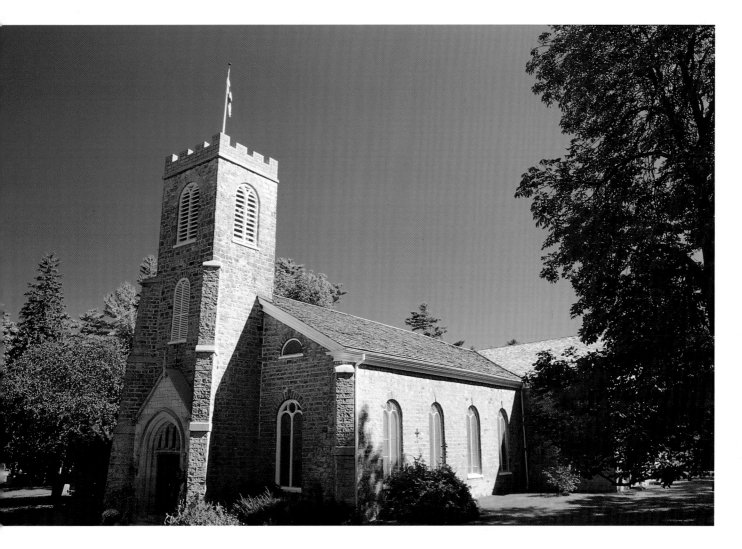

PRIDEAUX STREET

When peace came to the Old Town after the War of 1812, the entire waterfront district was in ashes. A determined populace re-built the town. Prideaux Street was a popular site and still bears examples of early postwar recon-struction.

One of the earliest homes is at *78 Prideaux (circa 1817)*. It shows the typical Georgian balanced facade, gable roof, end chimneys, simple transom light and small paned twelve-over-twelve windows.

Of similar Georgian design, *Promenade House* at *55 Prideaux (circa 1819)* was one of the many inns and taverns in the Old Town. A decorative transom crowns the entry. The walls are more than a foot (30 cm) thick and display Flemish bond brickwork on the two street faces.

Matching alcoves flank the elaborate pilastered mantel in the parlour of Promenade House. The fine china before the hearth, com-bining Chinese motifs with the Staffordshire rose, belonged to the first Postmaster General of Canada.

Demeath at *69 Prideaux (circa 1817)* was built for Dr. Robert Kerr. It was set close to the street on a narrow lot, with its gardens affording a view of the lake. The surgery was likely to one side with its own entrance, balancing the off-centre main entry. The rest-oration of Demeath included returning the main stairway to face the front door. An early owner is said to have reversed the stairs to prevent passersby from viewing the ankles of his daugh-ters as they descended the stairs.

Above: *69 Prideaux*

Below: *78 Prideaux*

Opposite page: *55 Prideaux*

PRIDEAUX STREET

New home construction boomed in the 1830's, an era of rapid growth and thriving commerce in Niagara. The family of Alexander Stewart, one of the first lawyers in Upper Canada, built the impressive Georgian home at *42 Prideaux (circa 1832)*. It boasts quite a distinguished facade, considering that it was built just one room deep.

Regency style brick arcading frames a balanced array of small paned windows in five bays. A magnificent classic portico complements the intricate fanlight and sidelights of the entry.

The home at *18 Prideaux (circa 1835)* shows many original local characteristics with its wooden clapboard finish, six-panel door, eaves returns, cornice gutters and small paned twelve-over-eight windows. Early glass making by hand resulted in window panes that were small and numerous. The upper sash usually had more panes than the lower when they were not equal in size. Larger glass panes became more popular as manufacturing techniques improved.

Burberry Cottage (circa 1830's) at *17 Prideaux* was a simple frame house with a three-bay facade. The typical Georgian entry was made off-centre by the later addition of a fourth bay.

An elegant board and batten home at *31 Prideaux (circa 1850)* has Greek Revival frets with pedimented trim above its windows and door. In the 1870's the mansard roof was added, as seen at Randwood on John Street and the Prince of Wales on Picton Street.

Opposite page:

Upper: *17 Prideaux*

Middle: *31 Prideaux*

Lower: *18 Prideaux*

This page: *42 Prideaux*

JOHNSON STREET

Following the War of 1812, Johnson Street was a popular location for home building. Clustered close to the main commercial street of town, the houses seemed a safe distance from the threat of another attack from the river.

The most prevalent building style of the time in Niagara was Georgian. Homes were rectangular with end chimneys, a balanced facade of regularly placed small paned windows and a central entry.

Many homes were painted white. A visitor to Niagara in 1827 noted the abundance of white frame houses, as found to this day throughout much of the Old Town. Contrary to common belief, white paint was an extravagance that was often avoided in favour of less costly mixtures tinted with yellow ochre, Venetian red or other colours still popular on the New England coast.

The earliest home on the street is at *96 Johnson (circa 1816)*. As is typical of urban Georgian architecture, it is set so close to the street that the front porch was removed to accommodate the sidewalk.

The home at *135 Johnson (circa 1822)* is similarly placed. Its wide chimneys serve four original fireplaces, two on each level. Though small in size, it was one of Niagara's many inns.

A carriage builder once operated a thriving business in shops adjacent to his home at *126 Johnson (circa 1828)*. Elegant mouldings and a plain transom light adorn this early Georgian style home.

This page: *135 Johnson*

Opposite page:

Upper: *96 Johnson*

Lower: *126 Johnson*

The *Clench House* at *234 Johnson* is undoubtedly one of the most handsome early homes in the Old Town. It was built by Ralfe Clench, a wealthy Loyalist from Schenectady, New York.

Clench was Niagara's first town clerk and rose to political distinction as a member of the Parliament of Upper Canada. He was active in the Masonic Lodge, St. Andrew's Church, the Niagara Turf (horse racing) Club, the Lincoln militia and Niagara Agricultural Society. Clench was a school trustee, a librarian and a judge, and he even operated an inn at the ferry dock.

The Clench home of 1807 was one of the fortunate few that survived the burning of the Old Town in 1813. It did burn, however, in an accidental fire a short time later.

The elaborate rebuilt home (1816-1831) is Neoclassical in style with typically balanced proportions, classical details and an elegant finish. Set on a grand two-acre lot, it faces the garden and the meandering One Mile Creek.

Fluted pilasters with carved Ionic capitals separate the five bays of the facade. A fanlight and sidelights distinguish the central entry and a Venetian window on the upper level surmounts the colonnaded portico. The white clapboard exterior conceals brick inner walls that were designed for warmth.

The interior craftsmanship is a delight with elaborate trim throughout. Colonettes, bat's wing friezes and carved elliptical fans adorn the fireplaces.

Both pages: *234 Johnson*

JOHNSON ST REGENT ST

Many homes sprang up along Johnson Street in the building boom of the 1830's. James Blain, a master mason and the contractor for St. Andrew's Church, operated a brick supply business from the rear of his home at *95 Johnson (1835)*. It became known as the *Post House* in the mid-19th century when it served as a post office. The entrance was likely at the corner as indicated by the brickwork repair.

The doorway is the focus of the late Georgian style Post House. Fine fluted pilasters support a semicircular fanlight with moulded trim. The year 1835 is carved in the wedge shaped keystone above.

The home at *58 Johnson (1833)* is of similar design with its balanced facade, hipped roof and elaborate entry. Splendid pilasters frame the fanlight, sidelights and six panel door.

In the same period, a very different style of home was built at *89 Johnson (1838)*. A simple transom light and a pilastered architrave with Greek Revival details distinguish the entry of the roughcast stucco home.

The *Angel Inn (circa 1825)*, tucked between Queen Street and Johnson Street by the old market square at *224 Regent*, has operated continuously as an inn and tavern throughout its history. The clapboard building has an off-centre door and a four-bay front.

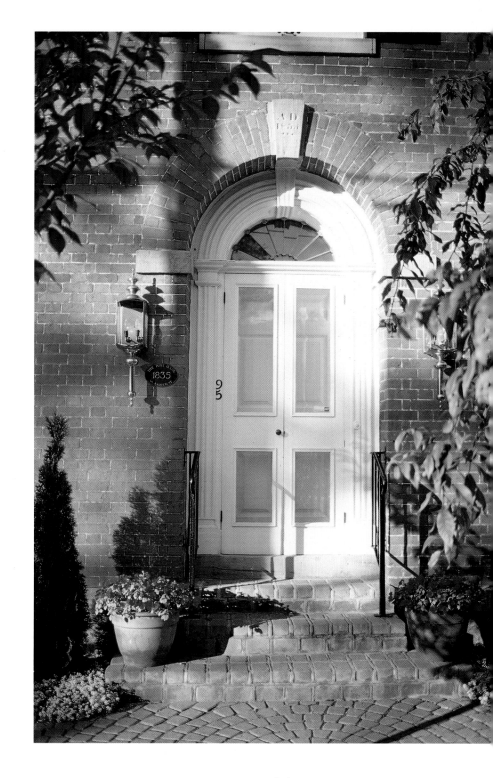

Above: *95 Johnson*

Opposite page:

Upper left: *89 Johnson*   Upper right: *58 Johnson*

Middle: *The Angel Inn*

Lower: *95 Johnson*

JOHNSON STREET

The *Sign of the Crown* at *118 Johnson (circa 1835)* was a typical tavern of the 1830's with a centre doorway as well as a side entrance for the tap room. It was built by Jared Stocking, the owner of a prosperous business selling fine hats, notably of beaver fur. Not too successful as a tavern, the simple Georgian style building became an evening school in the late 1830's and a boarding school in the 1870's.

Above the door of the Sign of the Crown is a black oval plaque, dated 1836, with a clasped hands insignia. It is an original fire in-surance marker, indicating that the owner had paid for the ser-vices of a private fire company to hasten to the building in the event of fire.

Nearby at *105 Johnson (circa 1837)*, George Varey, a tailor, had his workroom and shop in the northeast corner of his home. Its two-storey, three-bay, centre hall design is typical of buildings of the 1830's in Niagara. Sidelights, a plain transom and shutters call attention to the entry. The rough-cast finish and low hipped roof are late Regency style.

An unusual feature of window construction from 1840 to 1860 is evident in the home at *164 Johnson (circa 1845)*. The end panes of the front windows are just half the width of the centre panes. The home is typical of the Greek Revival style of the period. Narrow sidelights, a plain tran-som and moulded pilasters frame the central entry of the storey-and-a-half home.

Above: *105 Johnson*

Opposite page: Upper: *164 Johnson*   Middle: *118 Johnson*   Lower: *105 Johnson*

GAGE STREET

Still on the one-acre lot designated by the Surveyor General's survey of 1791, the Georgian style two-storey home at *83 Gage (circa 1830)* is known as the *White House*. The stucco walls are lined to resemble cut stone. Delicately patterned sidelights flank the door, but unlike most entries of the time, there is a simple entablature instead of a transom light above the door. The traditional centre hall leads to a parlour on either side and a rear wing was added in the 1880's.

The fine interior carpentry at 83 Gage is believed to be the work of John Davidson, who lived on Prideaux Street. The dining room is resplendent with its original mantelpiece set between alcoves decorated with prominent pilastered architraves, pointed arches and an unusual keystone design. The rocking horse is an American creation of the late 1700's.

Matthew Cathline, another carpenter and builder of the town, is credited with building the home at *58 Gage (circa 1840)*. Its fine doorcase with pilasters and sidelights is typical of the period.

The one-and-a-half storey clapboard home at *86 Gage (circa 1830's)* was built, like 58 and 83 Gage, at a time of rapid growth and commercial success in Niagara. Its gable end and main entry face the side garden. The home retains its original six-over-six window pane arrangement.

Above: *58 Gage*

Below: *86 Gage*

Opposite page: *83 Gage – The White House*

CASTLEREAGH STREET

In 1895 a group of prominent citizens led by Janet Carnochan met in the Court House to form the Niagara Historical Society. They ambitiously set about the task of collecting artifacts, publishing pamphlets and protecting the many historic sites in the town. Their activities led to the opening of the *Niagara Historical Society Museum* in Memorial Hall (1907), the first historical museum in Ontario built by a local society. This event preceded the opening of the Royal Ontario Museum in Toronto by five years.

The town of Niagara was the scene of many such historical precedents. It was the first capital of Upper Canada and site of the first Canadian parliament in 1792. The first census in Canada took place here and the first library appeared. Here, too, the first printing press operated and the first newspaper, the Upper Canada Gazette, was published in 1793.

In the mid-1900's the growing museum collection, housed in Memorial Hall, expanded into the nearby Grammar School (1875). A bridging section links the two older museum buildings. The eight windows in this central section were removed from the old parish hall (1886) of St. Mark's Church.

The museum's collection emphasizes the town's role in Canadian history. There is a significant collection of artifacts from the days of the United Empire Loyalists and the War of 1812.

Both pages: *Niagara Historical Society Museum –*

43 Castlereagh

MARY STREET
CENTRE STREET

William Duff Miller built the modest but charming home at *46 Mary (circa 1816)* for his wife and twelve children. A busy man, Miller was manager of a stationery store on Queen Street, an officer in the Lincoln militia, a strong supporter of St. Andrew's Presbyterian Church, and the Inspector and Deputy Clerk of the Crown and Pleas.

With its gable roof, end chimneys and five-bay centre hall design, the home is an excellent example of the Loyalist Neoclassic period. Seven fireplaces kept the family warm, with a corner fireplace in each of the four rooms upstairs. Typical of building construction in the decade following the War of 1812, all cavities between the interior and exterior walls were lined with brick, fitted from the inside before the lath and plaster were applied. The simple transom above the door is original.

The Regency style white roughcast-over-brick house at *8 Centre (circa 1835)* is unlike most early houses in Niagara. Chimneys dominate the centre of the front and rear walls of the square two-storey home and a garden in front sets the home well back from the street line. The off-centre entry is distinguished with a semielliptical fanlight, sidelights and an eight-panel door. The prominent shuttered windows left of the door are Regency "deceits", for they conceal a fireplace, not a window.

This page: *46 Mary*

Opposite page:

Upper: *8 Centre*

Lower: *46 Mary*

JOHN STREET

The Hon. William Dickson, a prominent Niagaran and Member of Parliament, built a two-storey Georgian manor house in 1793 on a large tract of land on the outskirts of town at *176 John*. Believed to be the first brick home in Newark, it was torched by American forces in 1813 while Dickson was a prisoner in Fort Niagara. As the legend goes, Mrs. Dickson, who was too ill to walk, was carried outside, bed and all, and left in the snow to watch her home burn.

Rebuilt on the foundation of the original structure, the grand home at 176 John retains its original elaborate doorcase with sidelights and fanlight. The mansard form of roof was added in the late 19th century when American summer residents expanded and altered the home. The dormer windows are typical of that period. George Rand, an American banker, named the home *Randwood*.

Brunswick Place, the lovingly restored Georgian brick home at *210 John (circa 1829)*, speaks of prosperity in the days of the booming shipyard industry in Niagara. It was built by Captain Robert Melville, manager of the Niagara Harbour and Dock Company, and then enlarged by American residents during the late Victorian period.

A lofty hipped roof with tall chimneys crowns a three-bay front. Colonettes, fine mouldings, a splendid fanlight and sidelights decorate the central doorcase, flanked on either side by wide windows. Stone quoins accentuate the brick corners.

Above: *210 John*

Opposite page:

Upper: *176 John*

Lower: *210 John*

WELLINGTON, DAVY & PLATOFF ST

The early Victorian saltbox home at *115 Wellington (circa 1850)* is believed to have been the home of United States Senator Mason following the American Civil War and the vacation retreat of Jefferson Davis, President of the Confederacy. Projecting wooden eaves and moulded fascia crown a brickwork facade of Flemish bond. Venetian windows flank the porch.

First owned by St. Mark's Anglican Church, the property was sold to raise funds to build the Rectory on Byron Street.

—

A shipwright built the home at *230 Davy (circa 1842)* when shipbuilding was the main local industry, employing 350 men. A single room on each side of the centre hall with the kitchen in a lean-to at the back was a common design in Niagara. However, unlike most local buildings of the era, it boasts long French windows and Victorian fretwork beneath the eaves.

—

The charming saltbox cottage at *20 Platoff (circa 1839)* was built on a lot only 30 feet wide and 50 feet deep (9 m by 15 m), just a fraction of the size of the one-acre lots in the central part of town and the half-acre lots near the waterfront. It displays simple plank shutters and a board and batten exterior, which was a typical finish of the mid-19th century.

This page: *20 Platoff*

Opposite page:

Upper: *115 Wellington*

Lower: *230 Davy*

KING STREET

John Graves Simcoe was the first Lieutenant-Governor of Upper Canada and a member of the Niagara Lodge, the first Masonic lodge in the province. The downstairs hall of the original two-storey building at *153 King* was the site of many of the town's social events and it may have been the site of the first Parliament. When the wooden building burned with the rest of the town in 1813, it was replaced by the existing *Masonic Hall (circa 1817)*, a large stone building set close to the street.

In the same period of postwar reconstruction, Indian agent William Claus built the low cottage known as the *Wilderness* at *407 King (circa 1816)*. The house is stucco, with lines cut to resemble stone. Its four-acre property, then on the outskirts of town, was a gift to his family from the Six Nation Indians. The mature historic garden of the Wilderness includes fruit trees, buttonwood and an outstanding gingko tree that is native of eastern China.

Lake navigators once used a tall poplar on the Wilderness property as a landmark. Arriving at the bustling dock area at the foot of King Street, sailors and visitors enjoyed the hospitality of the *Whale Inn* at *66 King (circa 1835)*. The two-storey clapboard building displays most of its original features, including a fine pilastered entrance with sidelights and shuttered six-over-six windows.

This page: *153 King – Masonic Hall*

Opposite page:

Upper: *407 King – The Wilderness*

Lower: *66 King – The Whale Inn*

KING STREET

A romantic tale is told of the home at *433 King (circa 1818)* that is called *Brockamour Manor.* It was built by John Powell, the county registrar, on the site of the family home that burned in 1813. Powell's sister-in-law, Sophia Shaw, is believed to have been the fiancée of Major-General Isaac Brock. It is said that the gallant Brock visited Sophia at the Powell home, even as he rode into battle in the early morning of October 13, 1812, just hours before his death at Queenston Heights. Brockamour Manor is a two-storey home with a hipped roof and small paned windows in three bays. The white stucco finish covering the original brick is a typical Regency feature in Upper Canada. It is jointed to resemble cut stone.

The small arcaded brick home at *708 King (1817)* was built in the years just after the War of 1812 as the town extended southwards. The medallion ornaments at the gable ends hint at the home's remarkably grand interior carpentry.

The home may have been the work of the same craftsman responsible for the neighbouring Court House and County Jail of 1816-1817. The grand building, with similar arcaded details, was used as a prison after the new Court House on Queen Street was built. In 1869, it became Miss Maria Rye's Western Home for orphaned and homeless girls from England. The home at 708 King was once part of the orphanage.

Above: *708 King*

Below & opposite page: *433 King*

KING STREET

King Street marked the edge of the surveyed town of 1791. The New Survey southeast of King was opened in the 1820's by James Crooks, a prosperous land developer. He had sold his lands around Fort Mississauga in exchange for more than 21 acres beyond King Street which he divided into very small lots.

As the area southeast of King began to develop, streets were extended but given new names, as often occurs in Great Britain. Queen Street crosses King to become Picton, Johnson becomes Platoff, and so on.

The home at *244 King (circa 1828)* may be the oldest in the New Survey. The two-storey, four-bay structure was once an inn and may have been a school at one time too. Typical of the period, it displays decorative cornices with eaves troughs hollowed out of solid wood moulding.

A more ornately decorated home was built later in the century at *177 King (circa 1885)*. The commodious two-and-a-half storey home is Queen Anne Revival style. It boasts a centre tower with a Saracen roof, intricately carved gingerbread trim on the spacious verandah, and fine detailing throughout.

A distinguished home of the same period but of simpler design is at *463 King (circa 1885)*. It belonged to the Lord Mayor of Niagara at the turn of the twentieth century.

Above: *177 King*

Opposite page: Upper: *244 King*   Middle: *177 King*   Lower: *463 King*

VICTORIA STREET

The simple Georgian home at *177 Victoria (circa 1816)* is an example of early postwar rebuilding in Niagara. With its original white clapboard, black door and shutters, and small paned twelve-over-twelve windows, it appears very much as it did when its first owner, John Wilson, a merchant, walked a short distance up the lane to Queen Street.

The door is the focal point of the balanced facade at 177 Victoria. The plain transom light is typical of the early Georgian style. To the right of the centre hall is the keeping room with its cooking fireplace.

The home at *315 Victoria (circa 1850)* is a modest home of the mid-19th century that follows the traditional Georgian style with its gable roof and balanced facade. A plain transom light, moulded trim, pilasters and sidelights distinguish the central entry.

Grace United Church (circa 1853) at *220 Victoria* was designed by William Thomas, the architect responsible for the Court House on Queen Street and Brock's Monument at Queenston. The founding congregation of the church was a group that broke away from St. Andrew's Presbyterian Church and became known as the "Free Kirk". Local Methodists purchased the church in 1875.

This page: *315 Victoria*

Opposite page:

Upper right, middle & lower: *177 Victoria*

Upper left: *Grace United Church*

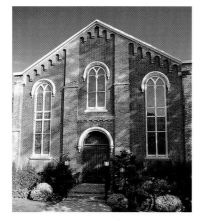

GATE STREET

The tiny dwelling at *243 Gate,* reputed to date to the 1820's, is known locally as the *Slave Cottage.* Its original tenants were free slaves, however, for an act of the Upper Canada legislature had abolished the importation of slaves in 1793. Many slaves from the United States travelled by the underground railway to Upper Canada where they found freedom and employment. Free slaves made up as much as one-fifth of the Niagara population by the mid-19th century.

The home at *240 Gate (circa 1818)* was once known as the "Shoemaker's Cottage". It originally had just one room upstairs and two below, but was extended on both levels in the 1840's. The clapboard covers walls of hand-made brick that may have been designed for warmth, and perhaps to defend against another bombardment such as the one suffered during the War of 1812.

The storey-and-a-half home at *223 Gate (circa 1840's)* was once the home of a harness maker. It is saltbox style with a long, rear sloping roof.

The *Methodist Meeting House (1830)* at *155 Gate* was first located three blocks away. It was moved in 1875 when the Methodist congregation decided to purchase the building that is now Grace United Church rather than continue the costly upkeep of their meeting house. The Georgian building has a balanced facade and a deep set centre door.

This page: *155 Gate*

Opposite page:

Upper: *243 Gate*

Middle: *223 Gate*

Lower: *240 Gate*

SIMCOE STREET

The simple yet distinguished home at *285 Simcoe (circa 1815)* may have once been the home of the famous Loyalist Colonel John Butler. It was moved from a site west of the Old Town to ensure its preservation. The original six-panel door and sidelights are trimmed with pilasters and fluted colonettes. The one-storey, five-bay clapboard with a hipped roof is of Neoclassical design.

A wealthy shipowner, banker and merchant built *Storrington* at *289 Simcoe (circa 1817)* on the foundation of a home from the previous century. Typical of early Niagara homes, it is a five-bay, two-storey, centre hall plan with a gable roof. The original brick is protected with stucco finished in a cut stone pattern. Storrington sits close to the street on the southeast corner of its original two-acre lot.

A storey-and-a-half saltbox style home at *322 Simcoe* was likely built between *1818* and *1826*. It directly faces St. Andrew's Presbyterian Church.

Creen House at *363 Simcoe (circa 1817-1825)* is the first of the homes built in Niagara by John Breakenridge, a Virginia lawyer. According to his obituary in 1828, he built "several of the most elegant and tasty houses in town".

Thomas Creen, rector of St. Mark's Church, used the home as a school in the mid-1800's and provided lodging for students. A lantern window on the peak of the roof lights the upper floor and staircase of the storey-and-a-half home.

Above: *322 Simcoe*

Below: *289 Simcoe*

Opposite page:

Both upper: *363 Simcoe*   Middle & lower: *285 Simcoe*

SIMCOE STREET

St. Andrew's Presbyterian Church at *323 Simcoe* is a handsome Georgian building with a magnificent Greek Revival portico. Massive Doric columns with fluted shafts mark the entrance. The original church of 1796 was burned by American forces in 1813 and rebuilt in 1831. The high wooden steeple was once used as a landmark and as a lookout post by both American and British troops. Through careful restoration work, the church interior and exterior appear very much as they did in 1831.

The church interior is a fine example of simple colonial ecclesiastical style. Splendid triple-hung windows with 24 panes each and a semicircular head rise skyward above rows of box pews, table pews and slip pews. Early parishioners paid pew rent, with the wealthy affording custom-built luxuries such as sloping or wider seats, extra shelves or footrests for their family pew.

The pulpit *(1840)* of black walnut is a fine example of the extraordinary craftsmanship of John Davidson. It is finished with decorative graining. The prominent overhead sounding board is crowned by a dove.

The *Manse (circa 1836)* at *342 Simcoe* reflects the classic Georgian style with its hipped roof and symmetrical facade. A fanlight and sidelights decorate the central entry to this home of rose coloured brick and cut stone. It was built by Dr. Robert McGill, a Minister of St. Andrew's, who provided a refuge for runaway slaves in the basement of the home.

Both pages: *St. Andrew's Presbyterian Church*

Above right: *342 Simcoe – The Manse*

MISSISSAUGA STREET

The *Hawley House* at *392 Mississauga (circa 1816)* is a magnificent home built shortly after the War of 1812. First owned by John Breakenridge, a lawyer from Virginia, the home was restored with meticulous authenticity by Frank Hawley, local champion of heritage preservation. Resembling the Federal style of New England, the home is Loyalist Neoclassical style.

Splendid fluted pilasters with Ionic capitals grace the white clapboard exterior. Pediments and modillion cornices decorate the gable ends. All are crafted from the native white pine that still grows on the spacious one-acre lot, among mature fruit, chestnut, black walnut, and butternut trees.

The spectacular doorcase is of intricate design. Panes of hand-blown glass in the embroidered fanlight and sidelights are joined by a tracery of cames with ornamental cast lead rosettes at the junctions.

The fine detail carries through to the interior of the *Hawley House*. The entrance foyer is a glorious reflection of the exterior. Throughout the home, delicately trimmed mantelpieces, fine mouldings and semielliptical archways reflect the early grandeur.

When Edward VII of England visited Niagara in 1876, he attended a ball at this home. As was his habit, he used his diamond ring to etch his signature in the glass of a built-in china cabinet in the dining room.

Both pages: *392 Mississauga – Hawley House*

MISSISSAUGA STREET

Like the Hawley House, the coach-house behind it at *392 Mississauga (circa 1816)* is authentically restored. It was used as a coach-house until 1899. The low building, with three carriage doors and living quarters above, accommodated the coachman and his family. Opposite the coach-house at the back corner of the one-acre property is a small cemetery where six free slaves were buried.

The rear ell extension at 392 Mississauga dates to 1830. At this time, the original scullery was moved from its place in the yard behind and attached to the main house. Rooms above the relocated kitchen provided lodging for servants. An original arched sunburst window over a built-in blanket box graces the upstairs hall.

Down the street from the Hawley House, Dr. Whitelaw's renowned private school once operated at *307 Mississauga*. It was one of several local schools that were based in a home, providing both tutoring and a dormitory for students. Built in *1818*, the home was extended in the 1830's with an ell on Gage Street that accommodated the school.

The prominent door with its original sidelights and pilasters is typical of early Niagara homes, but the asymmetrical design of the facade is unusual. The off-centre chimney serves back-to-back fireplaces on two floors and the original cooking fireplace in the basement.

This page: *392 Mississauga*

Opposite page:

Upper: *392 Mississauga – Coach-house*   Lower: *307 Mississauga*

South of the Old Town at *15927 Niagara Parkway* stands *McFarland House (1800)*, a handsome red brick Georgian home. It was built by John McFarland, who was "His Majesty's Boat-builder" in the reign of King George III. McFarland and his sons made all of the bricks for the home in a kiln on the estate.

Although it was the centre of much military activity during the War of 1812, the house was not destroyed. It was used as a hospital by the British and the Americans during the war and a gun battery was located on the property. Just days after the Americans torched the town of Niagara, British troops embarked from the ravine below McFarland House, making their way down the river to attack Fort Niagara at Youngstown. In an act of retaliation, the troops captured 29 cannons, 7000 muskets, 7000 pairs of shoes and a cache of clothing. Much of the booty had previously been taken from the British by the Americans.

Preserved as a museum, McFarland House contains some of its original furnishings, of the Empire period prior to 1840. The tall case clock in the dining room is fashioned of mahogany and figured maple.

In the early days of Upper Canada, a stage coach running between Niagara and Queenston regularly stopped to change horses at *Halfway House (circa 1800)* at *15540 Niagara Parkway*. The two-storey Neoclassical inn was built of local brick that was later covered with stucco.

Opposite page, upper: *15540 Niagara Parkway – Halfway House*

All others: *15927 Niagara Parkway – McFarland House*

Field House (circa 1800) proudly faces the road winding towards Queenston at *15284 Niagara Parkway*. It is one of the very few Niagara-on-the-Lake homes to survive the War of 1812. The two-storey brick Georgian home was built by Gilbert Field, a United Empire Loyalist from New Jersey and one of Butler's Rangers. His family maintained the home through the War of 1812 and for more than a century after. Similar in construction to McFarland House, it is a typical early Canadian home with a centre hall design and five-bay facade. A cooking fireplace is the heart of the "keeping room" where the Field family cooked and ate.

British Major-General Isaac Brock used the Field House as a military barrack in 1812. Later, the home served the occupying American troops as a hospital and barrack. Despite its distance from the shore of the Niagara River, it suffered bombardment by as many as five cannonballs fired from the American side.

The grand home nearby at *14902 Niagara Parkway (circa 1863)* was built in the quieter years of the mid-19th century, before Confederation. Peace had been made with the United States and the residents of Upper Canada were developing their own identity, a unique blend of British and American values and institutions.

Above: *14902 Niagara Parkway*

Below: *15284 Niagara Parkway – The Field House*

Opposite page: *The Field House*

Upper: *The Niagara River*

Lower: *15682 Niagara Parkway*

Opposite page: *15176 Niagara Parkway*

In the late 1700's, Lady Simcoe made many excursions along the bank of the Niagara River from her home at Navy Hall to Queenston and further south to the great falls. Her watercolour sketches depict the natural beauty of early Niagara. Homes sprang up along the beautiful winding trail that she travelled so often in her open carriage.

Stone was a preferred construction material for thrifty settlers, including the builder of the two-storey house at *15176 Niagara Parkway (circa 1835)*. Stones were gathered from surrounding fields in enough abundance to make the walls 26 inches (66 cm) thick. The home was the residence of Joseph Brown, the first peach grower of the area. It was also the birthplace of Calvin Brown, the first mayor of the nearby city of St. Catharines.

The house at *15682 Niagara Parkway* has a first floor stone foundation that may date to the late 1700's. The brick storey-and-a-half above was built following the War of 1812, as was most of Niagara that burned in 1813.

Although it came to be known as the *Priest's House* in the mid-19th century, its first owner was Isaac Swayze, the collector of taxes on all shop, tavern and still licenses. He reported the shocking invasion of his home by robbers in 1806 and the theft of more than 178 pounds of silver that he had collected for the public purse.

Sir Harry Oakes was a later owner of the Priest's House and kept his horses there.

Just north of the village of Queenston on the edge of the riverbank at *14795 Niagara Parkway* is the magnificent *Glencairn Manor (circa 1832)*. It overlooks the Queenston dock where its builder, John Hamilton, ran a prosperous shipping business. He built steamboats that ran between Queenston and Toronto (then known as York) and started the Royal Mail Line, connecting Niagara with Toronto, Kingston, and Hamilton. He was also a prominent Member of Parliament.

The Classic Revival style home has been compared to Thomas Jefferson's Monticello. Fluted columns with hand carved capitals grace the eastern facade, with spacious upper and lower galleries affording a spectacular view of the Niagara River and Lewiston. The home has 20 rooms, twelve fireplaces and two grand ballrooms. On the grounds of the estate are a carriage house and an old stone schoolhouse, that once served the children of the residents and the household staff.

Glencairn Manor surely bears some resemblance to the home of John Hamilton's father, Robert, the founder of Queenston. Thought to be accidentally burned by Upper Canada's own artillery during the War of 1812, the Robert Hamilton home at Queenston was described by Lady Simcoe, wife of the Lieutenant-Governor, as the finest home in Upper Canada, with a balcony running the length of the house and a wonderful view of the river.

Both pages: *14795 Niagara Parkway – Glencairn Manor*

QUEENSTON

British and Canadian forces clashed with American troops at Queenston Heights in the first major battle of the War of 1812. Major-General Sir Isaac Brock, provisional Lieutenant-Governor and commander of British forces in Upper Canada, lost his life in the assault.

Brock's Monument (1853) is a tribute to the legendary hero who is credited with saving Canada from American rule by gallantly storming the heights and urging his men on with the words "Push on, brave York Volunteers."

The monument, a symbol of the British way of life and Loyalist supremacy, had a stormy early history. The erection was halted at 48 ft (14.5 m) and torn down to remove from the cornerstone a copy of William Lyon Mackenzie's rebel paper, the Colonial Advocate. The second attempt was completed in 1824 but then destroyed in 1838 by a gunpowder blast that was set by a Mackenzie sympathizer. Rebuilt again, it stands 184 ft (56 m) tall. It is a Tuscan style monument, made entirely of cut stone, with lions and four figures of Victory at the base.

Legend has it that Brock's body was carried from the battlefield to the *Stone Barn (circa 1805)* at the rear of *17 Queenston*. Hand whittled wooden dowels secure the frame of the building.

The *Brock Memorial Church of St. Saviour (1879)* at *12 Princess* is the only Anglican church in the world that is dedicated to a layman. Its mixed congregation of Loyalists became Anglican in 1821.

Brock's Monument

Upper: *The Brock Memorial Church of St. Saviour*

Middle: *Brock's Monument Park*

Lower: *17 Queenston – Stone Barn*

QUEENSTON

Such famous Canadians as Laura Secord and William Lyon Mackenzie are part of the colourful early history of the Village of Queenston.

In 1813, Laura Secord overheard Americans in her home planning to attack the British forces at Beaverdams. Her legendary trek through 19 miles (30 km) of forests and swamps to warn British Colonel Fitzgibbon at DeCew made her a Canadian heroine. The simple frame home of Laura Secord at *31 Queenston* is a museum, restored to 1803.

In 1823, William Lyon Mackenzie opened a general store in his stately home at *1 Queenston*. The handsome limestone building is called the birthplace of responsible government, for Mackenzie soon turned his home into a printery to publish the "Colonial Advocate". The weekly paper expounded his rebellious views on the structure of the Canadian government. Late in 1824, Mackenzie moved to Toronto to continue his agitation for political reform.

Other early homes survive in the village. One of the earliest is the clapboard house at *48 Queenston (circa 1820)*. Another of the same period is the simple frame home built by George Wray at *25 Princess (circa 1820)*. It has stayed in his family for 175 years.

The *South Landing Inn* at *21 Front (circa 1827)* was an early inn. Its notorious owner during Prohibition was James Wadsworth, whose unlawful activities included bootlegging and smuggling immigrants across the Niagara River for fifty dollars each.

Upper: *31 Queenston – Laura Secord Homestead*   Lower: *1 Queenston – Mackenzie House*

Opposite page: Upper: *25 Princess;*   Middle: *48 Queenston;*   Lower: *21 Front – South Landing Inn*

QUEENSTON

The village of Queenston was a major port in the late 1700's and the first half of the 19th century. Robert Hamilton built wharves and storehouses and ran a thriving freight business. Salt, flour, guns and various goods were loaded onto wagons and hauled up the escarpment and around the falls. Furs arriving from the upper lakes were loaded onto ships bound for Montreal and overseas.

Hamilton built the red brick home at *93 Queenston (1807)* as a wedding present for his son, Robert Hamilton Jr. It survived the Battle of Queenston Heights in 1812 and remained in the Hamilton family for a century and a half.

Alexander Hamilton, the fourth son of Robert Hamilton, was a postmaster, judge and Sheriff of Niagara. He built the magnificent *Willowbank Estate (circa 1834)*. The 18-room home of Queenston limestone sits high above Queenston Street on a spacious 12 acres.

Willowbank Estate is a majestic Classic Revival home. Eight wooden Ionic columns rise two storeys high, flanking narrow processional steps that lead to the front door. Hand carved capitals, a pediment and classical mouldings enhance its grandeur. A sweeping spiral stairway graces the rear entrance.

The charming 19th century building at *36 Princess* is of heavy beam construction with limestone walls. While its date of origin is disputed, legend has it that it housed prisoners during the War of 1812 and illegal stores of liquor during Prohibition.

Above: *36 Princess*

Below: *93 Queenston*

Opposite page: *Willowbank Estate*

ST. DAVIDS

Forty homes and businesses burned to the ground when the New York State militia passed through the bustling village of St. Davids in 1814. One of the most influential members of that community was Richard Woodruff, a shopkeeper and Member of Parliament. He was known as "King Dick".

Woodruff built the Georgian clapboard home at *1385 York Road (circa 1815)* on the foundation of a home that had burned. Six original fireplaces survive, their pine mantels reflecting the Neoclassical influence. During restoration of the exterior, the carpenter's trademark coin, dated 1815, was found intact above a window casement, marking the date of construction.

The brick home known as *Locust Hall* was built for the Woodruffs at *1 Paxton Lane (circa 1824)*. The house has passed down through each generation to this day, now housing the fifth and sixth generation of the Richard Woodruff family.

Like the earlier Woodruff home on York Road, Locust Hall is a five-bay, two-storey home with a gable roof. Fan ornaments adorn the gable ends, sidelights and an elliptical fanlight frame the centre door, and stone quoins accentuate the corners. A carriage stoop borders the driveway.

The fine interior woodwork, as in the splendid drawing room mantel, is believed to be the off-season work of area shipwrights. In the dining room, portraits of early Woodruffs gaze down on a proud display of family heirlooms.

Upper, opposite page: *1385 York Road*

All others: *1 Paxton Lane – Locust Hall*

YORK RD
WARNER RD

Two handsome stone houses face the well travelled route between the villages of Queenston and St. Davids. They are Georgian homes with a gable roof, symmetrically placed windows and a centre hall plan. Although the Neoclassical style was replacing the Georgian style in the United States by the 1800's, many of the United Empire Loyalists in Niagara were conservative and clung to the Georgian design.

The storey-and-a-half home at *1717 York Road (circa 1820)* is one room deep in the main block with a centre hall and a kitchen ell in the rear. It was built by a sea captain, William Davis, on land purchased from the Secord family. Its plain doorcase is typical of early Georgian homes.

The two-storey home at *1755 York Road (circa 1820)* displays a similar design with its balanced five-bay facade, centre door and end chimneys. It has a more elaborate entry, however, as was typical of later Georgian homes. It was likely built by Loyalist David Secord, whose father, Peter, was granted 300 acres of land below the escarpment.

The remarkable fanlight crowning the door of 1755 York Road is a "deceit". The builder simply painted wood to appear as decorative window panes.

A splendid fanlight and colonettes elaborate the entry of yet another stone house at *287 Warner Road (circa 1837)*. The single storey, five-bay home was restored to its original appearance after many years of abandonment.

This page: *1755 York Road*

Opposite page:

Upper & middle: *1717 York Road*

Lower: *287 Warner Road*

LAKESHORE RD
FOUR MILE CREEK RD

The oldest surviving home in Niagara-on-the-Lake is *Lake Lodge (circa 1796)* at *1122 Lakeshore Road,* just west of the Old Town. It was built shortly after Reverend Robert Addison's arrival in 1792 as "Missionary to Niagara".

Addison is well remembered for sheltering the cold and homeless people of Niagara as they fled their burning town in December 1813. He is also recognized for bringing to Niagara his personal collection of 1500 books, which remains the oldest library in Ontario.

With its furnishings of the Georgian period, hand hewn beams and the interior paint treatment in its original bright colours, Lake Lodge evokes the period of Addison's life in Niagara from 1792 until his death in 1828. A country Chippendale style desk of native black walnut is typical of furniture made in the Niagara peninsula at the time.

A shallow Rumford style fireplace is the focal point of the master bedroom and of an upstairs meeting room. The Lake Lodge meeting room was likely used at various times as a chapel for Anglican services.

The handsome rural home at *1126 Four Mile Creek Road (circa 1805)* also survived the War of 1812. It was built by James Clement, a prominent early settler of the St. Davids area and an officer in the Lincoln militia. It is an early wilderness Georgian house that was updated in the 1830's with Neoclassical details as in the sidelights and semielliptical transom light of the doorcase, the eaves returns and the gable end fan ornaments.

Opposite page, upper: *1126 Four Mile Creek Road*

All others: *1122 Lakeshore Road – Lake Lodge*

Glossary of Architectural Terms

Architrave: moulding around a door or opening

Bay: a main division of a facade, indicated by a window or door opening

Board & batten: boards placed vertically with narrow strips covering the joints, often associated with a Greek Revival cottage

Bracket: a support for a horizontal projection, used to decorate cornices with increasing elaboration in the Victorian era

Cames: thin grooved lead rods holding panes of glass together

Clapboard: thin wood weatherboarding applied as an overlapping horizontal finish to a frame house

Classic Revival: an architectural style prevalent from 1830 to 1860, characterized by roof pediments, open porticos with fluted columns and Ionic capitals, and classical mouldings

Cornice: a moulded and projecting horizontal member that crowns a wall

Dormers: small windows projecting from the roof

Eaves: the lower border of a roof, sometimes projecting past the wall to form a cornice

Eaves returns: small horizontal extensions of the eaves at the gable end of a house

Entablature: a horizontal part that consists of architrave, frieze and cornice

Facade: the front of a building

Fanlight: a semicircular or semielliptical window with radiating muntins like the ribs of a fan, usually placed over a doorway

Flemish bond: a brickwork pattern with alternating stretchers (bricks laid lengthwise) and headers (bricks laid on end) horizontally and vertically

Fret: an ornamental work often in relief, consisting of straight bars intersecting at right or oblique angles

Frieze: the part of an entablature between the architrave and the cornice, often richly ornamented

Gable: the triangular end of a building from the cornice or eaves to the ridge

Gable roof: a roof with front and back slopes only, forming a gable at each end

Georgian: an architectural style started under Britain's King Georges and prevalent from 1785 to 1820, characterized by a symmetrical facade, centre door, rectangular openings, small paned windows and end chimneys

Gothic Revival: an architectural style prevalent from 1850 to 1870, characterized by symmetrical proportions, sharply pitched roofs, pointed arched windows, and intricately carved bargeboard with finials or drops at gable peaks

Greek Revival: an architectural style prevalent from 1830 to 1860, characterized by Doric, Ionic or Corinthian columns supporting an entablature and pediment

Hipped roof: a roof sloped on all four sides that may accommodate inside chimneys. Also called a cottage roof

Ionic: belonging to the Ionic order of architecture, characterized by a capital with volutes like rams' horns

Italianate: an architectural style prevalent from 1850 to 1870, characterized by square buildings with wide eaves and decorative brackets, square towers, roundheaded windows and a grand entrance

Keystone: a wedge-shaped piece at the crown of an arch

Mansard roof: a roof with two slopes on all sides, the lower slope being steeper than the upper, and often with a flat deck in the late Victorian era

Modillion: an ornamental bracket

Modillion cornice: a cornice with flat decorative horizontal brackets set close together

Moulding: a decorative strip used for finishing

Neoclassical: an architectural style prevalent from 1810 to 1930, characterized by balanced proportions, classical mouldings and details, a centre pediment and columns, and elegant finish

Palladian window: window with an arched centre piece and flat headed sides, named for the Italian Renaissance architect, Palladio

Pilaster: an upright rectangular column that usually projects just one-third of its width or less from the wall

Portico: a colonnade at the entrance to a building

Queen Anne Revival: an architectural style prevalent from 1885 to 1900, characterized by commodious houses with an asymmetrical arrangement of towers, bays and encircling verandahs, and a facade with a variety of textures, materials and colours

Quoins: alternating short and long pieces of brick or stone that accentuate the corners of a building

Reeding: a small convex moulding that appears corrugated

Regency: an architectural style that began in England in 1815, characterized by long verandahs, floor to ceiling windows, and small second floor windows, often approaching a square outline. Stucco was the preferred exterior finish

Roughcast: a stucco finish of rough texture formed by lime-encrusted gravel applied as a wet mixture against a wall

Rumford fireplace: a shallow style of fireplace with reflective walls

Saltbox: a dwelling with a two-storey front, a one-storey back, and a roof with a long rear slope

Sidelight: a narrow vertical window flanking a door or a larger window

Transom: a rectangular piece above a door or window

Transom light: the window of the transom

Venetian window: a wide, square headed window with a wide center light and narrow sidelights

Bibliography

Bassett, John M. *Elizabeth Simcoe.* Don Mills: Fitzhenry and Whiteside Ltd., 1974.

Blumenson, John. *Ontario Architecture.* Fitzhenry and Whiteside, 1990.

Boyle, Terry. *Under This Roof.* Toronto: Doubleday Canada Ltd., 1980.

Berton, Pierre. *Flames Across the Border 1813-1814.* Toronto: McClelland and Stewart, 1981.

Berton, Pierre. *The Invasion of Canada 1812-1813.* Toronto: McClelland and Stewart, 1980.

Campbell, Marjorie F. *Niagara - Hinge of the Golden Arc.* Toronto: Ryerson Press, 1959.

Condina, Cosmo. *Niagara-on-the-Lake.* North Vancouver: Whitecap Books Ltd., 1984.

Fink, Dean. *Life in Upper Canada 1781-1841.* Toronto: McClelland and Stewart, 1971.

Field, John L. *Niagara-on-the-Lake Guidebook.* Niagara Falls: Renown Printing Co. Ltd., 1984.

Fryer, Mary B. *Elizabeth Postuma Simcoe.* Toronto: Dundurn Press Ltd., 1989.

Greenhill, Ralph; Macpherson, Ken; and Richardson, Douglas. *Ontario Towns.* Ottawa: Oberon Press, 1974.

Heritage Property Files, Town of Niagara-on-the-Lake Planning and Development Services.

Hill, Nicholas. *Queen-Picton Street Area, Niagara-on-the-Lake: A Heritage Conservation District Plan.* London: Nicholas Hill Architect-Planner, 1986.

Innis, Mary Q., ed. *Mrs. Simcoe's Diary.* Toronto: MacMillan of Canada, 1965.

Macrae, Marion, and Adamson, Anthony. *The Ancestral Roof.* Toronto: Clarke, Irwin & Co. Ltd., 1963.

McBurney, Margaret, and Byers, Mary. *Tavern in the Town.* Toronto: University of Toronto Press, 1987.

Mead, Anne V. *Niagara-on-the-Lake.* Peterborough: Total Graphics Ltd., 1977.

Mika, Nick and Helma. *Niagara-on-the-Lake.* Belleville: Mika Publishing Company, 1990.

Ondaatje, Kim, and Mackenzie, Lois. *Old Ontario Houses.* Gage Publishing, 1977.

Seibel, George A. *The Niagara Portage Road.* Niagara Falls: The City of Niagara Falls, 1990.

Seibel, Olive M., ed. *Visitor's Guide to Ontario's Niagara Parks.* Niagara Falls: The Niagara Falls Heritage Foundation, 1979.

Stokes, Peter John. *Old Niagara-on-the-Lake.* Toronto: University of Toronto Press: 1971.

Stokes, Peter John. (Picken, H.B., and Wooll, G.R., ed.) *Early Architecture of the Town and Township of Niagara.* The Niagara Foundation, 1967.

Walker, Susan, and Herod, Dori. *Exploring Niagara-on-the-Lake.* Toronto: Greey de Pencier Publications, 1977.

Note: Cover Depiction of Royal Arms

The version of the Royal Arms depicted on the front cover was adopted when Queen Victoria took the throne in 1837. The royal shield displays the three lions of England, the single rampant lion of Scotland and the harp of Ireland. The English royal motto "Dieu et mon Droit" meaning "God and my right" was adopted by Edward III in 1340 and came into permanent use during the reign of Henry VI. The Garter's motto "Honi Soit qui Mal y Pense" also dates to Edward III. It is said that when the Countess of Warwick dropped a garter at a Court function, the King saved her from embarrassment by putting it on his own leg and remarking, "Shame be to him who thinks ill of it."

Index